Albert Fink

Railroad Accounts

And Governmental Regulation of Railroad Tariffs

Albert Fink

Railroad Accounts
And Governmental Regulation of Railroad Tariffs

ISBN/EAN: 9783744729208

Printed in Europe, USA, Canada, Australia, Japan

Cover: Foto ©ninafisch / pixelio.de

More available books at **www.hansebooks.com**

RAILROAD ACCOUNTS,

AND

Governmental Regulation of Railroad Tariffs.

By ALBERT FINK,

VICE-PRES'T AND GEN'L SUP'T OF THE LOUISVILLE & NASHVILLE
AND GREAT SOUTHERN RAILROAD.

*EXTRACT FROM THE ANNUAL REPORT OF THE LOUISVILLE
& NASHVILLE RAILROAD CO.*

LOUISVILLE:

PRINTED BY JOHN P. MORTON AND COMPANY.

1875

CONTENTS.

PAGE

Percentage of Net to Gross Earnings no Criterion of Economy. 4–8

How Railroad Accounts should be kept, and Explanation of
  Tables of Annual Report... 8–17

Classification of Operating Expenses..............................17–20

Causes of Difference in Cost of Transportation...................20–27

Comparison between Railroad and other Transportation..........27–29

Governmental Regulation of Railroad Tariffs......................29–31

Principles upon which Railroad Tariffs must be constructed......32–35

Just and Unjust Discrimination....................................35–40

Governmental Railroad Tariffs a Failure.........................40, 41

Prevention of Extortion and Unjust Discrimination..............41, 42

Contents of Tables of Annual Report..............................42–44

Estimates of the Value of Branch Roads to Main Line............44–46

Heading of Accounts...................... 47

Formula for Cost per Ton-mile....................................... 48

RAILROAD TRANSPORTATION.

The length of the roads operated during the year is as follows:

Main Stem... 185.00 miles.
Bardstown Branch .... 17.30 "
Knoxville Branch.. 110.32 "
Richmond Branch .... 33.46 "
Memphis Line .... 259.10 "

Total length of road owned by the company .... 605.18 "
Leased Roads—Glasgow Railroad.......................... 10.50 miles
            Nashville & Decatur Railroad......... 122.30 miles
                                                  132.80 "

Total length of road operated... 737.98 miles.

*   *   *   *   *   *   *   *   *

The following table may be of some interest, showing the number of tons of freight carried over the Main Stem and branches from 1865–66 to 1871–72, and over the Main Stem, branches, and Memphis Line from 1872–73 to 1873–74; also the gross revenue, cost, and net revenue per ton per mile, and the percentage of net to gross earnings:

MAIN STEM AND BRANCHES.

Year.	Length of Road—Miles.	Revenue per Ton-mile.	Operating Expenses per Ton-mile.	Profit per Ton per Mile.	Percentage of Net to Gross Earnings.	Ton-miles.
1865-66......	303.10	5.37	3.04	2.33	43.3	26,960,849
1866-67......	333.30	4.13	2.31	1.82	44.8	27,504,811
1867-68......	336.30	4.23	2.27	1.96	46.3	25,190,442
1868-69......	367.92	3.31	1.74	1.57	47.4	40,813,713
1869-70......	381.40	3.01	1.81	1.20	39.8	57,885,740
1870-71......	392.45	2.57	1.81	0.76	29.5	71,912,950
1871-72......	392.45	2.30	1.46	0.84	36.5	87,642,216

MAIN STEM AND BRANCHES AND MEMPHIS LINE.

Year.	Length of Road—Miles.	Revenue per Ton-mile.	Operating Expenses per Ton-mile.	Profit per Ton per Mile.	Percentage of Net to Gross Earnings.	Ton-miles.
1872-73......	605.75	2.21	1.60	0.61	27.6	141,649,448
1873-74......	605.75	2.11	1.41	0.70	33.1	128,434,191

From this statement it appears that since 1867–68 there has been a constant increase in the tonnage until last year. It also appears that during the period embraced in this statement there has been a constant decrease in the gross revenue, operating expenses, and net revenue per ton-mile.

PERCENTAGE OF NET TO GROSS EARNINGS NO CRITERION OF ECONOMY.

The information contained in this table illustrates the error which is often committed in using the percentage of the net to the gross earnings as a criterion of the economy with which a railroad is operated.

In 1865–66 the net freight earnings were 43.3 per cent and in 1873–74 only 33.1 per cent of the gross earnings. It would be erroneous to conclude from this that the road was operated with less economy in the past year. It will be observed that the gross earnings per ton-mile in 1865 were 5.37 cents; in 1874 they were only 2.11 cents. Had the gross earnings per ton-mile in 1874 been the same as in 1865, the net earnings would have been 74 per cent instead of 33.1 per cent of the gross earnings. It would, however, be equally erroneous to conclude that in 1865 less economy was exercised in the operation of the road than in 1874. The differences are accounted for by other reasons. In 1865 the bulk of the freight was local, carried over short distances of the road; since that time it has become mainly through business, which goes over the whole length of the road. The latter is transacted at less expense. Since 1865 the amount of business on the Main Stem has more than trebled. This increase causes a reduction in the operating expenses. There is a certain class of operating expenditures that do not increase with the amount of business; they are fixed expenses which have to be incurred whether a small or a large business is transacted. It follows that when only one third of the number of tons of freight were moved in 1865 as compared with 1874, the cost per ton-mile for this class of expenditures would be three times greater than in 1874.

In order to make a just comparison between the economy of operation in two different years, it becomes necessary to take into consideration the amount as well as the character of the business, whether through or local, and also the cost of labor and material prevailing during these years. But even then the comparison gives no correct results. We have further to discriminate between the expenditures made during one year due to that year's operation, and the expenditures made due to the operation of former years. The expenditures on account of renewal of rails, cross-ties, bridges, rolling-stock, etc., do not always, I may say hardly ever, represent the exact cost of making good the wear and tear caused by the business of the year in which they were incurred. For the first few years of the operation of a new road, for example, the expenditures on the accounts just named would be very small, and afterward they must become correspondingly large.

If we therefore fail to ascertain correctly the operating expenses for each year, the net earnings as shown in the annual reports for any one year do not form a proper basis for estimating the value of railroad property. The results of some years' operations lead to hope and others to disappointment, either of which may not be justified by the facts.

To illustrate this subject further, the following estimate of the expenditures during the year on the Main Stem of the Louisville & Nashville Railroad which are not chargeable to last year's business is submitted.

For Repairs of Iron Rails.—The gross ton-miles moved over the Main Stem during the year were 307,483,718. Taking the average number of tons of iron worn out by 100,000 gross ton-miles, as shown in Table XIX (0.95 tons), the amount of iron worn out by the last year's business was 2,921 tons. The actual cost of renewing this iron will be, including labor,

At $50 per ton...	146,050 00
The amount expended last year (Table II, items 42–45)	180,735 85
Amount not chargeable to last year's operation	$34,685 85

This estimate is based upon the average wear of iron. But there are now 72 miles of steel rails on the Main Stem: estimating their wear at four times that of iron and the cost $20 per ton more, we find that instead of 1,094 tons of iron only 273.5 tons of steel rails were worn out. The difference in cost of renewal amounts to

1,094 tons of iron at $50...	54,500 00
273.5 tons of steel at $70...	19,145 00
	$35,355 00

Total amount overcharged for repairs of rails in 1873–74, $70,240.85.

For Repairs of Cross-ties.—The cost of replacing cross-ties per year on the Main Stem since the road was first built has been, as per statement XX, $257.11 per mile.

The cost chargeable to last year's operation is 185×257.11................ 47,565 35
The amount actually expended on that account was (Table II, item 14).. 68,244 67

Amount not chargeable to last year's operation $20,679 32

For Bridge Repairs.—The average cost of bridge repairs for the last eight years has been $141.24 per mile per year. During the past year the expenditures on this account were unusually heavy, $250.26 per mile. The condition of the bridges is at present such that the cost of repairs will hereafter be much less than the average for the last eight years; but estimating it to be the same, the expenses incurred last year were greater than the average, 185 × (250.26 — 141.24) =$20,168.70, and the total amount for iron ties and bridges not chargeable to last year's operation is $111,088.87.

This large amount of money expended during the last year (as well as similar amounts in the two preceding years) was due to the operation of former years. In the coming year, on account of the excellent condition in which the road now is, these expenditures can be reduced at least to the average, if not below it, and large reductions will be made on account of the reduced wages and cost of material, so that we may confidently expect larger net earnings. It is fortunate that the heavy expenditure required to make good the wear of former years had been incurred before the effects of the panic of 1873 upon the business of the road were felt. In the near future we must expect the business of the company to be comparatively light. Fortunately no heavy expenditures will have to be made.

It will appear from what has been said above that it is impossible to judge of the economy of railroad operation from the annual reports of a railroad company for any one year without estimating the expenditures that are really due to each year's operation. Large net earnings may be shown in one and much smaller in another year, yet the road may have been operated with the same degree of economy in both years.

To make the annual reports of a railroad company of value, the accounts of the company should be so kept as to show the expenses due to that year's operation. For that purpose an account should be pened which might be called "renewal account," and to which hould be credited or charged the difference between the estimated ost of the operating expenses due to the year's work and the oper- ting expenses actually incurred during the year. This account would ave to be credited when the actual cost is less and charged when it ; more than the estimated cost. The balance of this account at the nd of the year will be a proper charge against the revenue account. t is true that these balances can only be estimated; but as railroad racks, ties, bridges, etc., are never made entirely new again, there lways will be a certain amount charged to this renewal account which ill represent the depreciation of the property, and the owner of the roperty will have a clearer idea of its value than if no such account ad been kept, although it may not be entirely correct.

I have purposely pointed out the difficulties encountered in forming orrect estimates of the economy of railroad operations, because, on ccount of the effects of the general stagnation in business upon the alue of railroad property, greater interest is felt in this subject than eretofore. It is surprising to find that so deceptive a criterion as he percentage of operating expenses to gross revenue is still used by 1any intelligent persons (among whom are not only stockholders, ut bankers and financiers) to judge of the economy of railroad perations.

In addition to what has been said as to the impossibility of basing ny judgment upon such data, the following table is submitted, which hows the percentage of operating expenses to gross earnings, also he revenue and cost per ton-mile and per passenger per mile on the everal roads operated by the Louisville & Nashville Railroad during he year 1873–74:

ROAD.	Percentage of Operat'g Exp. to Gross Earn-ings...	Revenue Ton-mile per	Cost per Ton-mile, exclusive of interest ...	Revenue Passenger per	Cost per Passen-ger, exclusive of interest ...
		Cents.	Cents.	Cents.	Cents.
. Main Stem.............................	63.80	2.037	1.32	3.56	2.50
. Glasgow Railroad	67.14	18.064	8.23	4.98	3.33
. Knoxville Branch	73.09	2.676	1.87	3.63	2.74
. Bardstown Branch......................	75.19	5.504	3.72	3.40	2.39
. Memphis Line.........................	76.49	2.014	1.44	3.88	3.20
. Nashville & Decatur Division......	78.38	2.605	1.74	4.13	4.34
. Richmond Branch......................	101.41	3.419	3.91	3.64	3.36

These seven roads from which the above results are obtained are
under the same management, and whatever may be the degree of
economy exercised in their operation, it is the same on all; yet the
proportion of operating expenses to gross earnings vary from 63.8 to
101.4 per cent, the cost per ton-mile of freight from 1.32 to 8.23 cents,
and per passenger from 2.5 to 4.34 cents.

HOW RAILROAD ACCOUNTS SHOULD BE KEPT, AND EXPLANATION OF TABLES OF ANNUAL REPORT.

If the percentage of operating expenses to net earnings, or the
cost of one ton of freight or one passenger transported one mile, can
not be used as an absolute measure of economy, or even as a measure
of comparison, and we have seen it can not, the question arises, What
is the proper course to pursue in ascertaining whether a railroad is
economically operated or not?

To this the answer must be given that the only mode of ascertaining this fact thoroughly is to make an examination of each item
of expenditure incurred in the operation of a railroad, and see whether
this has been reduced to a minimum and the service rendered for
it to a maximum. To make this investigation requires of course a
thorough and practical knowledge of railroad operations, of the cost
of material and labor, of the quality of the same, and of the best
results that can be obtained therefrom. But even that knowledge
would be of little avail unless the accounts of the operating expenditures of railroads are kept in such a manner as to exhibit in detail
not only the expenditures, but also the amount of work performed
for each item of expenditures.

In the annual reports of this company I have endeavored, as far
as practicable, to present the accounts of the expenditures in such a
manner and for the purpose set forth. I propose to call special attention to the information contained in this report, because of the great
interest which is now manifested in the subject of railroad transportation, and the necessity that both the owners of railroad property and
the people should possess correct information regarding it.

The tables accompanying this report may be divided into two
classes. The *first class*, from Table I to XXV,* contains statements of

---

* These tables are published in the Annual Report of the Louisville & Nashville Railroad
Company for 1873-74. The "Headings of Accounts" of tables II and III are printed on page
47 in this pamphlet, and should be referred to by the reader instead of these tables.

the operating expenses and statistical information regarding the same; the *second class*, from XXVI to XLV, contains statements of the amount and character of the freight and passenger traffic, with the revenue derived therefrom.

Table I contains in a condensed form, under one hundred and two heads for each road, the general results of the operation of the Main Stem and branches and leased lines, both as regards expenses and revenue.

Table II contains statements of the operating expenses under seventy-seven subaccounts for each road. The total sums expended on each account are shown in this statement; but from this no opinion can be formed as to the economy or judiciousness of the expenditure. In order to aid in analyzing the expenditures, with the view of forming such an opinion, the following tables are prepared, showing the expenditures for *certain units* of work performed.

Table III shows the expenditures per *mile of road* and per *train-mile*. The figures in the first column designate the same accounts as are indicated by the same figures in Table II. The items 1 to 29 show the cost per mile of road for maintenance of roadway, buildings, general expenses, etc.; items 30 to 74 the cost per train-mile.

There are some accounts, however, for which the cost "per mile of road" or "per train-mile" can not be used as a criterion of economy, because the expenditures on these accounts are independent of the number of miles of road operated or the number of miles run by trains. For this reason it becomes necessary to present these accounts in some other manner, so that they may show the amount and character of the work done, as well as the expenditures incurred. The following tables have been prepared for that purpose.

Table IV shows in detail the expenditures incurred at stations. The total amounts expended were shown in items 30 to 35, tables II and III. The number of tons of freight handled and the cost per ton at each station are shown in this table.

Station expenses form a very large proportion of the operating expenses of a railroad, and when their aggregate amount is only known it is impossible to tell whether this branch of the business was conducted with economy or not. But by showing the cost per ton of freight handled a measure is obtained by which a proper check can be put upon this class of expenditures. This, however, to

B

be of use has to be done from month to month, and for that purpose monthly statements are made out showing the cost of conducting the business at the principal stations.

Table V is such a statement, showing the cost per car-load of freight forwarded from and received at Louisville for each of the following items: Labor (loading and unloading freight), clerks (receiving and delivering freight), agents, cashiers, office-clerks, and watchmen (general expense); yardmen and switchmen; expenses of switching-engines.

With close attention to the management of the business of a station for a few months the minimum cost at which freight can be handled can be readily ascertained. This being known, it requires only some clerical labor in order to obtain a check over a very important class of expenditures, amounting on the Main Stem of this road to about 25 per cent of the total operating expenses, and of such a character that very little personal supervision can be exercised over the same.

Tables VI, VII, VIII, and IX show the cost of repairs of each bridge, depot-building, shop-building, water-station, and section-house on all the roads. The total amount of expenditures on these accounts are shown in Table II, items 15 to 19.

The expenditures detailed in these tables belong to that class which can not be tested as to their economy by using the mile of road operated or the number of train-miles run over it as a measure of cost. Hence the cost of the repairs of each individual structure is shown, from which, with a knowledge of its condition at the beginning and at the end of the year, an opinion can be formed as to the judiciousness of the expenditures. The tables of course contain only the total amounts expended on each structure. When further information is desirable the books, which contain accounts in detail with each structure, must be consulted.

While it is comparatively easy to trace the expenditures just named, and obtain a proper check over the same, it is more difficult to do so with another account, usually designated "road repairs."

The work performed in maintaining the roadway and track is of a complicated character, and in order to establish some unit of measure of cost and work it becomes necessary to classify the expenditures according to each special character of work, and apply the proper measure to each class separately. For that purpose the general account of road repairs has been subdivided in the reports of this company as follows (the figures indicate the same accounts as those in tables II and III):

42. Cost of renewal of rails; number of tons of rails used, and cost per ton.
43. Labor of replacing rails; number and weight of rails replaced, and cost per ton.
44. Cost of hauling material for renewal of track; tons of rails hauled; cost per ton.
45. Cost of joint-fastenings, spikes; cost of same per ton of new rails.
11. Cost of renewal of cross-ties; number of ties used; cost per tie.
12. Cost of labor replacing ties, per tie.
13. Cost of hauling ties, per tie.
1. Adjustment of track per mile of road.
41. Adjustment of track per train-mile.
3. Ditching per mile of road.
2. Repairs of ballast per mile of road.
7. Repairs of road-tools per mile of road.
6. Repairs of hand and dump-cars per mile of road.
9. General expenses of road department per mile of road.
10. Extraordinary repairs, slides, per mile of road.

I propose now to examine each of these subaccounts, and show which is the proper unit of measure to be applied to cost and work.

42. *The cost of renewal of rails* varies with the tonnage passed over the rails, the speed of trains, and the quality of the iron. To ascertain what should be the wear of rails under a certain usage requires careful observation during many years upon the different classes of iron in the track. The general results obtained during the last eighteen years on the Louisville & Nashville Railroad have been recorded in statement XIX, which will be referred to hereafter more fully.

From this statement it appears that on the Main Stem 100,000 gross tons passed over one mile of road wore out 0.95 tons of rail (60 lbs.), while on the Memphis Branch the same gross weight wore out 1.5 tons. On the Knoxville & Bardstown branches no deduction can as yet be drawn, as there has not been sufficient wear of the iron. The rails on the Memphis Branch were of the tubular form,

and proved in comparison with those on the Main Stem very inferior. By examining further the wear of each particular brand of iron
under the tonnage we find that of some brands only o.75 tons were
worn out by 100,000 tons of gross weight on one mile of road, while
of others 1.75 tons, showing a very great difference in the quality
of iron.

On account of this great inequality it is impossible to fix upon
any positive measure of wear and predetermine very accurately what
should be the cost per gross ton-mile or per train-mile for repairs of
iron. But, using the average result obtained from the experience of
many years, we may at least make approximate estimates. The most
valuable use to which the information obtained by keeping accurate
records of the wear of iron may be put is to aid us in selecting the
best quality of iron, to determine the best mode of manufacturing
it, and to decide when it becomes advantageous to use steel rails;
all of which are important questions in the economy of railroad
operation, which can not be intelligently answered without such
information.

The amount of money involved in selecting good or inferior iron
may be estimated on the Louisville & Nashville Railroad as follows:
The total gross tonnage that passed over all the roads operated by
this company in the past year was equal to 614,882,166 tons carried
over one mile. If the whole road was laid with the best iron that
we have used, there would be required per annum under this tonnage
4,611 tons of iron, and if with the most inferior iron which we have
used, 10,760 tons, a difference of 6,148 tons, which at the present
low price of iron, including labor of relaying—say $50 per ton —
would amount to $307,400.

The next item of expense incurred in keeping a road in repair is
the *labor of replacing rails*, the cost of which can be properly measured by the number of tons of new rails laid. The same holds good
approximately as regards the cost of *joint-fastenings, spikes*, and the
hauling of iron. If the minimum cost of these several classes of work
is once ascertained by special observation, a check over a large amount
of expenditure can be readily established.

Renewal of cross-ties (items 11, 12, 13, tables II and III).—The
average number of ties in one mile of road, the rate at which they
decay per annum, the minimum cost of ties, labor of replacing, and

hauling are the principal elements which determine the amount which should be expended per year on this account. The accounts of this company have been so kept as to exhibit all this information. The results of the experience for the last fifteen years regarding the durability of ties and the number required per annum, the cost of labor per tie, etc., have been recorded in statement XX.

Adjustment of track (items 1 and 41, tables II and III).—In this account is charged the cost of keeping the track in proper adjustment as regards line and surface, and necessarily includes the cost of bedding the ties for the purpose of sustaining the rails in their proper place. The cost of this work depends upon the nature of the road-bed, the action of the weather, and the amount and character of the traffic. In order to obtain a measure of economy we have to divide this account into two parts, in accordance with the cause which makes the expenditures necessary :

(*a*) The cost of bedding ties and adjusting track, so far as this work may be required, regardless of the extent of the use that is made of the road, depends on the character of the road-bed, the influence of climate, etc., and cost of organization for the purpose of attending to this work.

(*b*) The cost of re-adjusting track as far as made necessary by the passage of trains over it.

The proper measure for the expenditure referred to under (*a*) is the "mile of road," and under (*b*) the number of tons passed over the track, or approximately the number of "train-miles." The cost of this work must necessarily differ on different roads. No general rule can be adopted that will apply to all roads ; yet by an observation for several years in each individual case the minimum cost per mile of road and per train-mile for each class of work may be ascertained and used as a check upon this class of expenditures.

In tables II and III this account (adjustment of track) has been divided in accordance with the result obtained from observation made on this road during the last fifteen years. The cost per mile of road is shown in item 1, tables II and III, and the cost per train-mile in item 41.

The division of this account becomes also necessary when we desire to ascertain the relations existing between the cost of additional tonnage passing over the road and the cost that has to be incurred independent of the tonnage—an important item in estimating the cost of transportation.

3. *Cost of ditching* differs with the nature of the soil, climate, and amount of rainfall. With observations extending over a number of years the minimum cost per mile of road may be approximately ascertained in each individual case, and may be used as a check on this class of expenditure. The same may be said of the cost of repairs of ballast (2), road-tools (7), repairs of hand and dump-cars (6), and general expenses of road department (9).

The *cost of extraordinary repairs* includes the cost of repairing damage to road-bed caused by freshets, slides, etc. These are accidental causes, hence no measure can be applied to this except that based upon experience for a great number of years.

This analysis of the various subaccounts which are usually comprised under one general account, called "road repairs," shows how impossible it is to apply to the general account one measure—such, for example, as the "mile of road" or "train-mile"—and use it to ascertain the economy with which the work was done, or to make comparison between different roads. The many elements of cost of different nature must be separately considered and compared. Thus we could not compare the cost of adjustment of track of a mile of road over which forty trains pass with the cost of a mile over which only one train passes without separating the expenses incurred on account of tonnage from those which are independent of the tonnage.

We have now ascertained the various accounts from 1 to 46, tables II and III, and established proper measures that can and should be applied to each, to determine the judiciousness of the expenditures. We will now proceed to examine the other accounts from 47 to 73.

Table XI shows the cost per train-mile and engine-mile in detail of the following items named in tables II and III :

        48. Locomotive repairs.

        49. Oil and waste used on locomotives.

        50. Watching and cleaning.

        53. Engineers and firemen's wages.

        63. Fuel used by locomotives.

48. *The cost of locomotive repairs* may be measured approximately by the mile run, yet it is necessary to examine into the cost of repairs

of each individual locomotive in order to determine the economy with which the work was performed. Detailed accounts are therefore kept with each locomotive.

53. *Engineers and firemen;* 55. *Conductors and brakemen.*—The elements determining expenses on these accounts are the wages paid to each class of employees per day, and number of miles to be run by them constituting one day's work. The total expenses under this account should not exceed the cost per mile so ascertained, multiplied by the total number of miles run.

49 and 63. *Oil and waste and fuel* used by locomotives can be readily checked by the number of miles run. It is necessary to ascertain from direct observation the most economical results that can be secured under existing conditions, and apply it as a measure to the whole year's work.

The expenses for fuel form so large a portion of the operating expenses of railroads that accurate accounts must be kept of the consumption of each engine, and these accounts must be balanced with the total amount of fuel bought. Without such check the detailed statement can not be relied upon as correct. Inventories of the fuel on hand are taken every six months, and all the fuel bought is fully accounted for.

Table XII contains a yearly balance-sheet of fuel account, in which is shown the amount of fuel bought and consumed during the year, and for what purpose used, cost of same, etc.

Table XIII. *Car repairs.*—The unit of comparison of this work is the number of miles run by the several classes of cars. This table contains the mileage made by each class of cars, and cost of repairs per mile. The expenditures shown in items 66–72 depend principally upon accidental causes, and no fixed measure of economy can be adopted for the same.

I have now examined the several items constituting the operating expenses of the road, and in a general way pointed out the mode in which the accounts should be kept in order to enable the managers to obtain proper checks and control over the expenditures, and to aid others in the investigation of the economy with which the road has been operated. There are some additional tables attached to this report which give details of expenditure and other statistical information relating thereto, to which I will now refer.

Tables XIV and XV are balance-sheets of the iron- and brass-foundry accounts, showing the amount of castings made, material bought, cost of making castings, and material and castings on hand July 1, 1874.

Table XVI shows the operating expenses of the steamer "Dick Johnson" on the Tennessee River. This steamer was put on the Tennessee River to secure business from that river which we could not obtain otherwise, with the view of increasing our tonnage in the direction in which it is now lightest, adding to the revenue without much additional expense. Satisfactory arrangements have been made with the E. & T. P. Co. to run in connection with our road after July 1st, and from that time the company will discontinue to operate its own steamer.

Table XVII shows in detail the amount expended for new rolling-stock acquired during the year, and for other improvements which have increased the value of the road, and which are not properly chargeable to the operating account.

The following tables contain further statistical information.

Table XVIII shows the cost of road repairs per mile of road and per train-mile from the time the roads named were completed or came into the possession of this company until the present day; also the amount of new iron used during each year.

Table XIX shows the cost of renewing iron on four roads since their construction; also the number of tons of gross weight due to the passenger and freight traffic passed over the iron since it was laid. This tonnage is given in three different modes: 1. The actual gross tonnage passed over the road, including switching and construction service; 2. The gross weight of passenger and freight revenue-trains alone; 3. The gross weight of the freight revenue-trains, and double the gross weight of the passenger revenue-trains. It is presumed, as data for comparison, that the wear of one gross ton of a passenger-train moved over the iron at double the speed of a freight-train is equal to the wear of two gross tons of a freight-train. In order to ascertain the wear of iron by the tonnage passed over it from the time the iron was new up to the present time it is necessary to take in account the depreciated condition of the iron at present and the estimated cost to make the track new again. These estimates are shown in this table, and the results obtained have been referred to before (page 11).

Table XX shows the number of cross-ties used on the various roads since their construction up to date, the cost of same, the cost of labor relaying and hauling per tie. It was also necessary to make the estimates of the number of ties required to make the road new, as the average number of ties used per year up to this time does not represent the full wear of the ties per year.

Table XXI shows the amount of new iron laid during the past year, and quantity of each kind of iron and steel in the road on July 1st.

Table XXII shows the condition of the road-bed as regards ballast.

Table XXIII shows the length of side-tracks.

Table XXIV shows the number and kind of cars and locomotives owned by the company.

Table XXV shows the value of materials on hand July 1st. This is the last table of the report containing information in regard to the operating expenses.

CLASSIFICATION OF OPERATING EXPENSES.

Before leaving this subject attention is called to the classification of accounts in tables II and III. It will be observed that the accounts are divided into three classes:

> Maintenance of road, buildings, and general expense, from account 1 to 29.
>
> Station expenses, from account 30 to 40.
>
> Movement expenses, from account 41 to 74.

The expenditures of each class bear a distinct character, to which I will now refer more particularly.

Those in *the first class* are not affected by the amount of business transacted, within certain limits to be referred to hereafter. The roadway must be kept in good order. Cross-ties when decayed must be renewed, bridges kept in repair, and a certain organization of officers and men must be kept up, whether one or more trains are to pass over the road.

This class of expenditure per mile of road will vary on different roads according to the permanency of construction, the number of bridges to be kept in repair, the nature of the soil, the climate, and many other local conditions. They will also vary with the amount of business, but only to the extent to which an increase of business requires more extensive accommodation, such as depot - buildings, side-tracks, etc., which have to be kept in repair. On a road with an established business, and having suitable accommodation for the same, considerable variation in business may take place without affecting this class of expenditures.

The *second class* of expenditures are incurred at stations in keeping up an organized force of agents, laborers, etc., for the purpose of receiving and delivering freight, the selling of tickets, etc.

One portion of these expenditures does not vary with the amount of business; another portion does. A certain number of agents have to be employed, whether there is more or less work to be done; but the number of persons employed to handle freight may be varied in proportion to the number of tons of freight to be handled. This whole class of expenditures, however, is entirely uninfluenced by the length that either freight or passengers are hauled, or, in other words, by the work of transportation performed. Freight or passengers may be hauled five or two hundred miles, the station expenses incurred on their account being the same.

In the *third class* of expenditures have been collected all those that vary with the number of trains run.

On roads on which there is sufficient freight business to fill all trains that are run from one terminus of the road the amount of freight transported will be nearly in proportion to the number of freight train-miles; and hence on such roads this third class of expenditures will be nearly in proportion to the amount of business. It is this class of expenditures alone which possesses that characteristic.

On roads, however, upon which freight-trains have to be run at stated times, whether fully loaded or not, this class of expenditures does not vary with the business, but very nearly with the number of trains run. The expenditures and amount of freight transported in this case are irrelative, the cost of transporting freight being dependent entirely upon the loads as accidentally offered for transportation.

To the three classes of expenditures just named, and which have been shown separately and in detail in tables II and III, must be added a fourth, not shown in these tables, but which forms a large proportion of the total operating expenses of railroads—viz., the interest on the capital invested.

This class is mainly uninfluenced by the amount of work done. Only so far as an increase of business involves the necessity of additional investments for its accommodation is it influenced by the amount of business.

In the consideration of the subject of the cost of railroad transportation it is of the greatest importance to discriminate between the expenditures which vary with the amount of work performed and those which are entirely independent thereof. The latter form so large a proportion of the total operating expenses of railroads that it becomes impossible to make the *amount of work performed* a criterion or measure of the cost.

The fixed or inevitable expenses which attach to the operation of railroads, and which are the same whether one or many trains are run over a road, have to be ascertained separately in each individual case. These expenditures are in the nature of a tax upon the business of the road ; the smaller the business the larger the tax. What the tax may or should be per ton of freight or per passenger carried in any one case can not be predetermined by any general rule or law, but can only be ascertained after the two elements on which it depends— (1) the fixed expenditures, and (2) the amount of work done—are actually known. These elements vary on all roads; it would be a singular accident to find them alike on any two.

The disregard of these facts in estimating the cost and the value of railroad transportation with a view of judging of the reasonableness of railroad tariffs has led to many erroneous conclusions, which appear to be now fixed in the public mind. It is of great importance to the owners of railroad property at this present time—more so perhaps than heretofore—to possess correct information upon the subject of the cost of railroad transportation. It may therefore not be considered out of place here to show how the cost of transportation varies upon the various roads operated by the Louisville & Nashville Railroad, and the reasons therefor.

The following table (A) shows the percentage of the four classes of expenditure above referred to, of the total operating expenses on the seven roads operated by the Louisville & Nashville Railroad Company.

TABLE A.

	M. S.	M. L.	N. & D.	K. B.	B. B.	R. B.	G. B.
Movement expenses	41.367	38.589	38.594	22.428	19.490	17.634	28.761
Station expenses	18.161	12.924	12.259	4.367	6.209	5.832	5.007
Maintenance of road	14.453	17.179	17.554	17.964	22.505	17.295	9.361
Interest on investment	26.019	31.308	31.593	55.241	51.796	59.239	56.871
Total	100.000	100.000	100.000	100.000	100.000	100.000	100.000

From this table will be seen the great diversity existing in the relative proportions of each class of expenditures. ·

The movement expenses, the cost of conveying freight from one place to another after it is loaded in the cars—the transportation expenses proper—are 41.3 per cent on the Main Stem, and only 17.6 on the Richmond Branch, of the total operating expenses. We have therefore in one case 58.7, in the other 82.4 per cent of the total operating expenses, which are entirely uninfluenced by the amount of work performed as measured by weight and distance, or ton-miles.

The station expenses vary from 4.3 per cent on the Knoxville Branch to 18.1 per cent on the Main Stem of the total operating expenses.

The cost of maintenance of road is 9.3 per cent on the Glasgow Branch, and 22.5 on the Bardstown Branch.

The interest account is 26 per cent on the Main Stem, and 59.2 per cent on the Richmond Branch.

With such great variations in the constituting elements of the cost of transportation uniformity in the final results can not be expected.

CAUSES OF DIFFERENCE IN COST OF TRANSPORTATION.

I will now compare the expenditure of each class per ton-mile on the seven roads, and show more particularly the reasons for the great difference in cost.

The following table (B) shows each class of operating expenses per ton-mile on the seven roads operated by the L. & N. R. R. Co.

TABLE B.

COST PER TON-MILE.	M. S.	M. L.	N. & D.	K. B.	B. B.	R. B.	G. B.
	Cents.	Cents.	Cents.	Cents.	Cents.	Cents.	Cents.
Movement expenses	.7365	.8102	.9787	.9364	1.5039	1.6934	5.4928
Station expenses	.3233	.2714	.5109	.1823	.4791	.5601	.0563
Maintenance of road	.2573	.3607	.4451	.7499	1.7366	1.6608	1.7877
Total operating expenses	1.3171	1.4423	1.7347	1.8686	3.7196	3.0143	8.2368
Interest	.4633	.6574	.8011	2.3061	3.9968	5.6887	10.8615
Total oper'g exp. and interest	1.7804	2.0997	2.5358	4.1747	7.7164	9.6030	19.0983

Movement expenses (comprised of items 41–73, tables II and III).—
It appears that on the first four roads this class of expenditures varies
from .73 cents to .97 cents per ton-mile; on the last three named from
1.50 cents to 5.49 cents per ton-mile. The first four roads belong to
that class on which fully loaded freight-trains can be started from one
terminus of the road; on the last three named trains are started at
regular times, regardless of the amount of load that is to be carried.
Hence we find greater agreement in the cost of moving one ton one
mile on the first four roads than on the latter, on which the cost
depends altogether upon accidental causes.

If on the first four roads the grades, curves, and the cost of labor
and material were the same, and also the character of the business,
then the cost per ton-mile should be the same; but as these elements
of cost differ, uniformity in the cost even in the movement expenses
can not be expected.

The character of the business of a road has a great influence upon
the cost of transportation.

We find the average train-loads carried on the first four roads, and
the movement expenses per ton-mile, as follows:

	M. S.	M. L.	N. & D.	K. B.
Average train-loads ....tons	135	113	96	77
Movement expenses per ton ....cents	0.73	0.81	0.97	0.93

On the Main Stem the average net load carried per train is nearly
twice as much as on the Knoxville Branch.

On the first-named road a large amount of freight is carried over
its whole length; while on the latter, which is a mere local road, it
only passes over a portion of its whole length. The capacity of the
locomotive and train can not therefore be as fully utilized on the latter
as on the former road.

On the Main Stem the tonnage in one direction is 73 per cent of
the tonnage in the other direction, while on the Knoxville Branch it
is only 21 per cent; hence more empty cars have to be run on the
latter than on the former road.

The result is that an average of 135 tons of freight is being carried
per train on the Main Stem, while only 77 tons can be carried on the
Knoxville Branch; yet the same attention is paid on both roads to
secure maximum loads to each train.

It is the character of the business peculiar to each road that brings about this great difference, which of course influences the cost of transportation.

On roads on which there is not sufficient business to secure full loads to the trains from one or the other of the terminal stations the difference in the movement expenses per ton is found still greater.

The following table shows the average loads carried in the trains of the three branch roads, and the cost per ton-mile for moving the freight :

	B. B.	R. B.	G. B.
Average number of tons freight carried on one train............	18.2	24.0	4.9
Movement expenses per ton-mile ....cents	1.5	1.7	5.5

It is on account of the small loads carried on the Glasgow Branch per train (4.9 tons) that the movement expenses are so much larger than on the other branches, on which the trains carry from 18.2 to 24 tons.

Station expenses (items 30–40, tables II and III).—The elements controlling the cost per ton-mile for station expenses are—

(*a*) The cost of handling one ton of freight—for loading, unloading, clerking, agents' salaries, depot expenses, switching, etc.

(*b*) The length of haul.

Supposing that the cost of handling freight per ton were the same on all roads and at all stations of a road, then the cost per ton-mile of freight would vary according to the length of haul. For each particular length of haul there would be a different cost per ton-mile for this service.

By reference to Table IV it will be seen that the average cost of station expenses per ton of freight handled on the Main Stem of the road is 23 cents. For freight that passes over the whole length of the line, say between Louisville and Memphis, the cost per ton-mile would be $\frac{2 \times 23}{377} = 0.12$ cents, and for freight carried only five miles it would be $\frac{2 \times 23}{5} = 9.2$ cents. We have therefore a difference between the cost per ton-mile from 0.12 to 9.2 cents, although the actual cost of performing the work was the same in both cases; thus showing that the ton-mile is not a proper unit of measure of cost of this service.

But there is even considerable variation in the cost of handling one ton of freight at various stations, as will appear from an examination of Table IV, which shows the station expenses per ton and the number of tons of freight handled at each station. We can ascertain from this table, in connection with Table XXVII, the average cost per ton-mile of freight handled at each station.

The latter table gives the number of ton-miles of freight received and forwarded from each station. Dividing the number of tons into the number of ton-miles gives the average haul, and dividing this into the cost per ton for handling gives the average cost per ton-mile for handling freight.

For example, take Brooks Station. Number of tons of freight received and forwarded (Table IV), 654; freight to and from Brooks Station was carried 14,335 miles (Table XXVII); therefore the average haul $\frac{14,335}{654}=21.8$ miles; station expenses per ton at Brooks Station (Table IV), 71 cents; cost per ton-mile $\frac{71}{21.8}=3.26$ cents. To this has to be added the expenses at the station from or to which the freight was forwarded.

If both stations are known, the cost per ton-mile for station expenses can be readily ascertained from Table IV. For example, for freight shipped between Louisville and Brooks Station, distance 9.2 miles:

Station expenses at Brooks Station per ton .... 71.0 cents.
Station expenses at Louisville per ton... 24.3 "

Total cost per ton... 95.3 "
Length of haul, 9.2 miles; cost per ton-mile, 10.4 cents.

This example sufficiently illustrates the great variety in cost, and the impossibility of making the ton-mile the measure of cost of or compensation for this service. The ton handled would be a more correct measure, although there is necessarily much variety even in this cost, as we have seen, and as will still further appear from an examination of Table IV.

It must therefore be evident that it is impossible to predetermine the cost per ton-mile of freight for handling without taking into consideration the length of the haul and the conditions under which the station service has to be performed.

Maintenance of roadway and general expense (items 1–29).—The two elements that determine the cost per ton-mile for this service are—

1. The cost of maintaining one mile of road, etc., during a given time.

2. The number of tons of freight passed over it during the same time.

The former differs on each road, and so does the latter; hence uniformity in cost per ton-mile is impossible.

The following table shows the cost of maintenance of roadway and general expense per mile of road on the seven roads operated by the Louisville & Nashville Railroad Company during the last year, and the average number of tons of freight passed over one mile of each road; also the cost per ton-mile:

	M. S.	M. L.	N. & D.	K. B.	B. B.	R. B.	G. B.
Cost of maintenance of road per mile per year (Table III, item 29)	$1,857.87	$1,142.25	$1,243.49	906.76	436.69	436.61	262.73
Tons of freight passed over one mile of road...................................	433,662	152,273	143,378	72,456	11,538	16,656	6,137
Cost per ton-mile...................cents	0.26	0.36	0.44	0.75	1.74	1.66	1.78

Part of the cost of maintenance of roadway and buildings is chargeable to the passenger traffic. The division of charges between the two classes of traffic has been made in proportion to train-miles. It follows from this that the cost per ton-mile of freight is in a measure affected by the relative use made of a road by the passenger and freight traffic.

From this statement will be noticed the great difference in cost of maintaining one mile of road, buildings, etc. On the Main Stem this cost is $1,857.87, on the Glasgow Branch $262.73 per mile.

An examination of the items from 1 to 28, Table III, will show in what particulars these differences occur. A few may be mentioned here. The cost per mile on the Main Stem and Glasgow Branch is as follows:

	M. S.	G. B.
Renewal of ties...	368.89	32.96
Bridge superstructure	250.26	25.14
Ditching..	69.23	26.06
General expense	346.14	....
Salaries, insurance, and taxes	100.40	....
Total...	$1,134.92	$84.16

The difference in cost in these five items on the Main Stem and Glasgow Branch is $1,050.76 per mile of road. Part of this great difference is caused from the fact that on one road greater expenditures were made during this year than was due to the year's business; on the other road less. It will be remembered that the yearly depreciation of cross-ties on the Main Stem was found to be for 16½ years at the rate of $257.11 per mile, while during the past year there was expended $368.89 on the Main Stem, and on the Glasgow Branch only $32.96 per mile; the first sum more, the latter considerably less than is required to make good a year's depreciation.

There are great differences in other expenses, such as repairs of bridges, on the two roads. On the Main Stem, as has been mentioned before, the cost of bridge repairs during the last year was unusually heavy, while on the Glasgow Branch, with only one small bridge, the cost is very small. The general expenses of administration on the Main Stem are not incurred on the Glasgow Branch, which is also exempt from taxation. Hence the great difference in cost of maintenance of road and buildings and general superintendence between the two roads.

When we examine into the differences existing in regard to the amount of business transacted in one year over one mile of road—the other element named which enters into the cost of one ton per mile—we find the variation still greater. On the Main Stem 433,662 tons, on the Glasgow Branch only 6,137 tons, pass over one mile of road per year. We can therefore not be surprised that the cost on the Main Stem for maintenance of road is only one fourth of a cent per ton-mile and on the Glasgow Branch 1.8 cents.

Interest account.—The original cost of the road and the rate of interest form one element and the amount of business transacted the other which determines the cost per ton-mile.

The cost of roads per mile and the business transacted over the same vary so much that the cost per ton-mile for interest can not be expected to be the same in any two cases.

It is impossible to predetermine what is a proper charge for interest on any particular road until these elements—viz., the cost of road and the amount of business—are known.

On the Main Stem of the Louisville & Nashville Railroad, dividing the number of ton-miles of freight carried into the interest chargeable to the freight business, the cost per ton-mile is 0.46, while on the Richmond Branch it is 10.86 cents, over twenty times as much. On the five other roads the interest charge varies from 0.65 to 5.7 cents per ton-mile. (For further particulars refer to Table B, page 20.)

We have now considered the variation in each class of expenditures and the causes therefor per ton-mile. When we find so much variation in the elements which make up the cost of transportation we can not expect to find uniformity in the total cost.

From Table B it appears that the variation in the total cost per ton-mile is from 1.78 cents on the Main Stem to 19.09 cents on the Glasgow Branch. The work performed—viz., the movement of one ton of freight one mile—is the same on all roads, yet the cost of performing is ten times more on one road than on the other.

Great as this variation is on the seven roads under the same management, the variation of the cost per ton-mile is still greater even on the same road, depending as it does upon the different conditions under which the service has to be performed. It would lead here too far to thoroughly analyze the cost of railroad transportation in all its details, and I will only state that a careful investigation shows that under the ordinary conditions under which transportation service is generally performed the cost per ton-mile in some instances may not exceed one seventh of a cent and in others will be as high as 73 cents per ton-mile on the same road. The lower cost applies to freight carried in cars that otherwise would return empty; the higher cost to freight in small quantities carried short distances.

It is impossible to predetermine the cost of carrying freight on any one road unless the conditions under which it is to be carried, as far as they affect the cost of transportation, be previously known.

In order to estimate the cost of transportation under the various conditions that occur it is necessary to classify the expenditures, and to separate those that increase with the amount of work done from those that are fixed and independent of it; and to ascertain the ratio of increase of cost with the increase of work. Without such an analysis of the cost it is impossible to solve the question of cost of transportation that arises in the daily practice of railroad operation. A mere knowledge of the average cost per ton-mile of all the expenditures during a whole year's operation is of no value whatever in determining the cost of transporting any particular class of freight, as no freight is ever transported under the average condition under which the whole year's business is transacted. We can therefore not make the average cost per ton-mile the basis for a tariff, if it is to be based upon cost; but we must classify the freight according to the conditions affecting cost, and ascertain the cost of each class separately.

A formula is given on page 48, showing the various elements entering into the calculation of the cost of railroad transportation.

COMPARISON BETWEEN RAILROAD AND OTHER TRANSPORTATION.

The problem of ascertaining the cost of railroad transportation is not quite so simple as it may at first sight appear. It is much easier to determine the cost of wagon, canal, or steamboat transportation. The common carrier by wagon or canal knows the exact amount of toll he has to pay, and assumes no risk of an investment in an expensive roadway. Nature furnishes a roadway to the carrier by steamboat, and keeps it in repair free of charge. Hence in estimating the cost of transportation by wagon, canal, or steamboat two of the most uncertain and changeable elements, and at the same time the costliest, of railroad transportation are eliminated from the calculation. Railway companies are not only *common carriers;* they are also *proprietors of a roadway.* Their tariff charges are not only for transportation service proper, for the service rendered as common carriers, but also for the *use of the roadway, for its maintenance, and for the risk assumed in the investment.*

Notwithstanding this distinctive character of railroad service, as compared with that performed by other common carriers, it is sought to regulate the tariffs of railroads and to judge, compare, and criticise the same by the same measure or rule that applies properly only to the service of common carriers; viz., the measure of *weight of freight and distance to which it is carried.* The idea prevails that the cost of transportation of a ton of freight on one railroad should not materially differ from that on others, and that the cost of moving freight should be in exact proportion to the distance to which it is carried.

These rules might be applied with some degree of justice to the cost of *moving* freight, although even here discrimination between different roads and different lengths of haul must be made; but the measure of weight and distance—the ton-mile—can not be used as a measure of cost incurred by railroad companies as *proprietors of the roadway.* This service must be measured by different rules. The cost of the roadway, the rate of interest and discount in obtaining money, the cost of the maintenance, and the actual use made of the roadway form the proper data for calculation.

On the seven roads operated by the Louisville & Nashville Railroad Company the cost of maintenance of road and interest on investment, when distributed over the number of ton-miles carried over the roads, is as follows (see Table B, page 20) :

	M. S.	M. L.	N. & D.	K. B.	B. B.	R. B.	G. B.
Cost per ton-mile ......cents	0.7206	1.0181	1.2462	3.0560	5.7334	7.3495	12.6492

This statement shows the great difference in cost, from 0.7 cents to 12.6 cents per ton-mile, although the service rendered is exactly the same: the use of the roadway for one mile for the purpose of moving over it one ton of freight.

Were these roads owned by one party and used by another (the latter common carriers merely), the toll, or the charge for the use of the roadway, would have to be made according to these figures, in order to reimburse the proprietor for the cost of the service. If the common carrier would then charge separately for his services for moving the freight by the ton-mile, and for handling, warehousing, and taking care of it by the ton, the difference between the charges for the service as common carriers on the different roads would not be so great.

If the charges for railroad transportation were thus subdivided, the reasonableness of the same could be more readily explained and understood. The confusion which exists in the minds of some people on the subject of railroad tariffs arises from the prevailing practice of combining the charges for three distinct services in one, and applying a measure to the whole which only can properly be applied to a portion of it.

So strong has become the conviction in the public mind that there should be uniformity in the cost of railway transportation that it has found expression in some of the states in legislative acts enforcing uniformity in compensation, while the natural laws governing cost, causing, as we have seen, so great a difference, are allowed to operate undisturbed.

The ton-mile, without further inquiry as to its adaptability, is made the measure of cost. If by comparing the tariffs of different roads, or the tariff for different services on the same road, a difference be discovered, the road charging the higher rates stands convicted of practicing extortion and unjust discrimination.

Upon such evidence as this laws have been enacted in some states for the purpose of preventing extortion, and which affect injuriously railroad property and the rights of a great many innocent people.

GOVERNMENTAL REGULATION OF RAILROAD TARIFFS.

It can not be denied that a law forcing railroad companies to furnish the use of their roads and to transact the business of a common carrier for less than cost is simply a law of confiscation, no matter under what pretext of authority it is enacted. It can hardly be maintained, in the light of our knowledge of human nature, that at the time the contracts between some of the states and the builders of the roads were made the latter were given to understand, as distinctly and clearly as they are now made to understand, that the state reserved the right to confiscate their property at pleasure. It appears that the interpretation of the law by one party to the contract was a great surprise to the other, originating as it did many years after the contract was made, during which time the construction now put upon it was not thought of or sought to be enforced. In ordinary cases the true meaning of a contract, if not unequivocally expressed, is determined from the manner in which the same has been executed through a long period of time; but this does not seem to hold good when railroads are parties to the contract.

The question as to the right and the extent of the right of the government of a state or the national government to prescribe fixed compensation for specific transportation services, or to regulate in a more general manner the railroad tariffs, is one of great interest and importance to all owners of railroad property.

The relations of the Louisville & Nashville Railroad Company to the states in which it is located are well defined by the several charters; yet the national government, at least one branch of it, has lately claimed jurisdiction over railroad tariffs, on the plea of having the power under the constitution to regulate commerce between the states; and there prevails a general tendency in the public mind that something must be done in the way of railroad legislation.

In the last legislature of the state of Kentucky a law was passed through the Senate making it obligatory on all the roads in the state to carry way freight (including the cost of handling it) at a rate not exceeding 25 per cent over the lowest rate per mile charged at the same time for through freight. A full explanation of the chartered rights of the company, and of the bearing and effect of such a law upon the railroads of the state and upon public interests, was made to the intelligent committees of both legislative branches, and this was sufficient to prevent the final enactment of that law.

In the legislature of the state of Tennessee several laws on the subject of railroad tariffs passed through one and some through the other branch of the legislature, and only failed at the close of the session for want of time.

These laws were of such a character that had they passed, and could they have been enforced, would have ruined the whole railroad property of that state.

It is true that such legislation could be clearly proven illegal and void, both under our charters and under the constitutions of the states, yet during the time required to do so great losses might be inflicted upon the stockholders, and expensive and troublesome litigation would follow. All of which can be avoided by a more thorough knowledge of the subject on the part of the people and their representatives. It can be readily shown that many of the difficulties of what is called the railroad problem are only apparent. They have their existence in the ignorance of the people upon this subject, and as soon as the facts appear in their full and true light most of them will vanish without the aid of legislative interference.

It is with a view of bringing about a clearer and better understanding of railroad transportation that I have referred to it in this report at so great length.

Nine tenths of the stockholders of the Louisville & Nashville Railroad and its leased lines are citizens of the states in which their roads are located ; the question of legislative control of railroads in this instance is not a mere party question between the people and "soulless corporations," but it is a question between the people who furnish the transportation and the people who use the roads. To a great extent they are the same, a great portion of the road being owned by cities and counties. A careful study therefore by the people of the facts and questions involved becomes almost a matter of necessity in the preservation of their own property.

The subject of legislative enactments regarding the tariffs of rail-roads not owned by the government must be considered in two aspects—first, as to the abstract right of the government to establish tariffs; and second, as to the practicability of establishing and enforcing the same so as to accomplish the object for which the control is undertaken.

The first question is one of law, and must be decided by the courts in accordance with contracts, charters, and constitutions; but the second is a question for the consideration of experts in the management of railroads, and must be decided from a knowledge of the facts and the natural laws controlling the subject.

Should the courts decide that the government has the right to establish or control railroad tariffs, and it be found in the nature of the case that the exercise of that right necessitated the violation of other fundamental laws, the question as to the abstract right would become of secondary importance.

There is a decision on record that bears upon this subject. It is not reported in the law-books, but has been universally approved. A certain citizen of Venice was given the right under the law to take one pound of flesh from a fellow-citizen. He found it impossible to obtain it without also taking blood, and probably life, to which he had no lawful claim; and the judgment therefore remained unexecuted.

The right of the government to establish and enforce railroad tariffs does not carry with it the right to confiscate the property of railroad companies. If a tariff can not be established and enforced unless the property of railroad companies is used without due compensation and without their consent, then this right ought not to be exercised, unless it be contended, as it has been by some, that "might is right." But even then it would soon be discovered that to deal unjustly with railroad companies will react sooner or later injuriously upon the public interest, and that to act in accordance with the dictates of justice in this as in all other cases will prove the best policy.

The question as to the right and policy of governmental interference with railroad tariffs practically resolves itself into this question: whether it be possible for the legislature to undertake this control without the violation of other laws and the rights of parties interested, and in such a manner as to fully accomplish the object for which this control is undertaken. This question I will now consider.

PRINCIPLES UPON WHICH RAILROAD TARIFFS MUST BE CONSTRUCTED.

The first principle that should guide the formation of railway tariffs stands written in the good book—"the laborer is worthy of his hire." Those furnishing transportation for others should be reimbursed for at least the cost. Had this principle not been recognized at the time the roads were built, few would now be in existence, and if it is to be repudiated now, few will be constructed hereafter. The proper basis of railroad tariffs is therefore the cost of the transportation service.

I have shown in this report the great variation in the cost of railway transportation on different roads, and the causes which necessarily bring about this result. From it necessarily follows the impossiblity of enacting general laws establishing tariffs applicable to *more than one road.*

What is reasonable compensation for railway transportation service, or what constitutes just or unjust discrimination in railway charges, is not a question that can be decided *a priori*, or that can be formulated into a general law. It can only be decided in each individual case, when all the conditions under which the service is performed and the elements controlling its cost are known; in most cases it can only be decided correctly after the service has been performed.

It would be just as sensible to predetermine by legislation what shall be the cost of raising a bushel of corn as to predetermine the cost of carrying a ton of freight. The action of the sun and rain upon the growth of the corn and the quantity of the yield are no less uncertain elements than some of the elements which enter into the cost of transportation service.

The average cost of moving one ton one mile on the Main Stem of the Louisville & Nashville Railroad is 1.78 cents; on the Glasgow Branch 19.09 cents. What justice would there be in establishing a law requiring both roads to work for the same compensation? Nor would it be more just to classify the railroads and enact a special tariff for each class, as no general laws exist or have as yet been discovered under which such classification could be made; the various combinations of elements of cost are different on and peculiar to each road, controlled as they are by local causes.

The great difference in cost referred to in this report occurs in the average cost per ton-mile of transportation during the period of a whole year; but there is still greater difference in the cost of transportation of one ton one mile on the same road, varying with the conditions under which the service is performed, according to the length of haul, the quantities in which freight is transported, and whether the freight is carried in cars that would have to return empty or in special trains. I have mentioned that according to these and other conditions it may cost one seventh of a cent only in some cases and seventy-three cents in others to transport one ton of freight one mile.

The labor therefore of forming a tariff based strictly upon cost is very intricate, and not of such a character that it can be properly performed by legislative bodies as at present constituted. The only mode in which they could act would be to appoint competent officers, whose duty it would be to ascertain the cost of transportation on each individual road, and to establish a tariff accordingly. If this duty could be properly performed, few railroad companies would complain, as the majority work for less than cost.

A tariff so established strictly upon the basis of cost would, however, be of little use unless it be accompanied by a law forcing the people to ship over the road a *certain quantity* of freight at the *established rates*. If they are left free to select other modes of transportation that may be cheaper, then it would soon become apparent that the railroad would be of use only to a very limited number of people ; as the number of shippers is decreased, the cost of transportation would be increased in many cases to such an extent that the turnpike would furnish a cheaper mode of transportation. *The fact would soon become evident that railroad tariffs can not be based upon the cost of transportation alone.* Other elements enter into their formation that can not be ignored, if it be intended to develop fully the usefulness of railroad property both to its owners and to the public. .

The question that greatly controls railroad tariffs is *what is the service worth*, not *what does it cost;* and this is a mere commercial question, uncontrollable by acts of legislation. The relative value of an article at the place from and to which it is shipped determines the charges for transportation it can bear. If a greater charge is made than the difference in these values, the article can not be moved. It

may therefore become necessary to charge on some articles less than
the full cost of transportation in order to enable it to be moved at all;
and this necessitates again to charge more on others which can bear
higher charges.

An element is here necessarily introduced of a purely commercial
character, and which requires a knowledge of the value of articles in
the different markets of the country between which they are to be
exchanged, situated often far beyond the limits of any one state.
This element must necessarily work constant changes in tariffs, and
it would therefore be impossible to predetermine the same or fix them
by legislative action.

There is another disturbing element that prevents fixed railroad
tariffs. *It is competition.* The simple question requires to be answered, Will you carry freight and passengers for the *same* that other
transportation lines charge, either by rail or river, or will you *not carry
them* at all?

All that has to be known by the railroad manager to answer this
question is the minimum cost at which the service can be performed.
If the obtainable rate exceeds cost, no matter how little, it becomes
his interest to accept the terms offered. The important question to
be decided is what is the minimum cost?

In the statements I have given on page 20 the average cost of
transportation per ton-mile for four different classes of expenses were
given. Two of these classes are not affected by the work done, but
are fixed; viz., the cost of maintenance of road and the interest on
the investment. On the Main Stem of the Louisville & Nashville
Railroad they amounted to 0.72 cents per ton-mile, or 40 per cent of
the whole cost, and the expenses for moving and handling freight were
1.06 cents per ton-mile.

Now it follows that when freight is to be carried at a rate fixed
by competition, and can not be carried at all if a greater rate is
demanded, the Louisville & Nashville Railroad Company can carry
the same at the rate of 1.06 cents per ton-mile, and not lose thereby;
if it could obtain more, the additional receipts would be just so much
profit, applicable to lowering the rate on other freight. Yet if the
Louisville & Nashville Railroad Company was to be forced by law to
do all their business at this low rate, the expenses would exceed the
income by 40 per cent, and the road could not be operated at all.

The company would prefer to abandon the competitive business and arrange the tariff for way business, by charging, when this is possible, as much more as the profit on the competitive business would have amounted to.

From this it will be seen that the transaction of this competitive business, apart from the indirect benefits which it may exercise, is more to the advantage of the shipper whose location does not give him competitive privileges than to the railroad company.

Notwithstanding this fact, the carrying of competitive freight at low rates is the most fruitful source of complaint on the part of the shipper who pays higher rates. It has given rise to the charges so commonly preferred against railroad companies of making unjust discriminations in their tariffs, and against which legislative protection has mainly been invoked.

JUST AND UNJUST DISCRIMINATION.

It is maintained that to carry freight between distant competitive points at lower rates than between intermediate points where no competition exists is an act of injustice to the shippers at the latter points. This conclusion is based upon the assumed principle that common carriers are bound to serve their customers alike. The application, however, of a general principle to complicated transactions, such as take place in the business of common carriers, without taking into account *all* the facts bearing upon the same, is apt to lead to erroneous conclusions, as it does in this case.

I will illustrate this subject by a special case which is a representation of many. Louisville and Memphis are connected by navigable rivers, and in the exchange of commodities between the two cities they have always had the benefit of low rates of river transportation. A railroad 377 miles long is built connecting the two cities, passing through a number of interior places, which had before only imperfect communications. Suppose one of these places, called A, be located on the line of this road, 100 miles from Memphis and 277 from Louisville; how is it affected by the construction of the road? Before the road was built freight from Louisville destined to A was shipped to Memphis by river and then by wagon to A. Since the road has been built there are two routes from Louisville to A, one by river to Memphis and thence by rail, and the other by rail direct to A. Taking the first route, the charge for shipping to A is made by adding to the river rate from Louisville to Memphis the rail rate for 100 miles from Memphis to A. This latter rate is much below the rate formerly charged by wagon, and to the extent of this difference the shipper at A has been benefited by the construction of the road, not to mention the greater convenience and saving in time of which he now gets the benefit. This ought and would be satisfactory if the road stopped at A; but the fact that a new route is opened to him, direct from Louisville, only 277 miles, causes all the trouble.

The railroad is obliged to carry freight from Louisville to Memphis at the low river rate, which is much below the average cost of railroad transportation; but it derives from this rate a small profit, for reasons fully explained on page 34. It is obliged for the same reasons to charge its customer at A more per ton-mile for the distance of 277 miles than is charged to Memphis; but this can in no case exceed the sum of the river and rail rates from Louisville to A *via* Memphis, for if it did, the latter route would be the preferred one.

Now the fact that the railroad carries freight from Louisville to Memphis through A at a lower rate than it carries it from Louisville to A is considered an act of injustice to the shipper at A, and he demands that he be put on the same, or even a better, footing with the shipper at Memphis, who always had the advantage of lower rates of transportation before the road was built. His demand amounts to this, that the railroad company having expended millions of dollars in the construction of a railroad connecting the interior places, which were without the improved modes of transportation, with two cities upon navigable rivers, conferring thus a great benefit upon those interior places, shall, in consideration of having done so much, do still more, and secure for them the same advantages possessed by the places situated upon the banks of navigable rivers.

It is rather surprising that some courts have decided this position to be right. They have declared it unjust discrimination for railroad companies to charge higher rates of transportation to intermediate than more distant points, a decision based upon the improper application of the principle that common carriers must not make any distinction among shippers.

From the foregoing illustration it will appear that discriminations necessarily have to be made; but it will also appear that it is not the common carrier who creates the same arbitrarily, but the nature of things makes them necessary. To pursue another course than that indicated would result to the disadvantage of all concerned and benefit no one. Were the low competitive freight to be refused, the cost of carrying other freight would be increased. If the same rate was to be charged to all interior points as to the competitive points, the railroad could not be operated at all.

Different localities are more or less favored in regard to transportation facilities, either by nature or the enterprise of man. It can not be maintained that it is the duty of the common carrier to equalize these existing inequalities at his own expense. All that is required of him is not to create them himself arbitrarily. He must treat all alike that are situated alike; but he can not be bound to wipe out existing differences. He may be obliged to carry freight at a lower rate to some localities than to others, but this in itself does not constitute an injustice or injury to the shipper in a less favored locality, as long as the charges made are reasonable in themselves and alike to all in the same situation.

Discriminations are the necessary result of competition, and competition is the best protection against extortionate charges—much more efficient than any artificial legislative device. To take away the right from railroad proprietors to establish their tariffs upon the recognized principles that guide all other commercial transactions, and substitute fixed tariffs or arbitrary rules on which they must be based, would destroy the great usefulness of railroads.

It may be and has been asserted that the effect of competition is not felt upon way business for which no direct competition is possible. This, however, is an erroneous view. When there is competition at any one point upon a railroad it makes itself felt over some portion of the road, more or less, according to the situation of the competing line. The truth of this can be illustrated by again referring to the case already cited. The rate from Louisville to an intermediate station on the road from Louisville to Memphis is established, as I have shown, by adding to the river rate to Memphis the railroad rate from Memphis to this intermediate station, which I have called A. The rail rate is limited by the charter, which prescribes maximum rates, or where this is not the case it would be limited by the consideration as to what constitutes a reasonable compensation for 100 miles of rail transportation, and could in no case exceed the rates charged for transportation by other modes that might be available from Memphis to A. It is therefore the competitive river rate from Louisville to Memphis that influences and establishes the rate to this interior point.

As the number of competitive points is multiplied on any one road the rates to a greater number of interior points are influenced, and this to a greater extent. Thus the Memphis Line from Bowling Green, where it diverges from the Main Stem to Memphis, 259 miles in length, is crossed by two navigable rivers and four other railroads, establishing thus six competing points. The shippers over this line can therefore always avail themselves of the competitive rates to the nearest point. They can in no case be charged more from Louisville direct to any station of the road than the competing rate and the rate of the short rail haul added, no matter what may be the distance from Louisville to the interior point. The consequence is that all the interior points enjoy the benefit of whatever competition there is; but it also follows that the tariff upon such a line can not be constructed upon a mileage basis, but must make more or less discrimination between the different localities according as they are affected by competition. It may necessarily require freight to be hauled over a longer distance for much less than it is carried for a shorter distance. It is either this or the abandonment of competitive business.

If railroad companies could agree among themselves to stop competition to junction points, one of the most fruitful causes of complaint against discrimination in railroad tariffs would at once be remedied; but it would be at the expense of the benefit of competition.

The same result must follow if the rates to competing points are determined by the legislature of the state in which they are situated. But in this case competitors by river and railroads in other states should also be compelled to maintain these rates; otherwise the roads over which the state has complete control could not do business at all at competing points. Surely the people could not be benefited by such a course; it would be much better to let the natural laws of competition have their full force. To interfere with them is certainly not to regulate but to obstruct commerce, for which there is no authority in the constitution of the United States.

The problem of establishing a railroad tariff that possesses all the desirable requirements is one not of easy solution. It is an intricate and difficult problem; but the more complicated we find it to be, the more reasonable it is to assume that it can better be solved by those who are directly interested, who practically devote their whole time and attention to it, than by members of a legislature, a majority of whom may be presumed to be utterly ignorant of this special subject.

It is generally supposed that the right to establish their own tariffs gives great power, liable to abuse, into the hands of railroad managers, but upon closer investigation it will be found that the extent of this power is generally much overrated. Enlightened self-interest dictates its exercise reasonably, and in a spirit of liberality; competition, especially with water transportation, circumscribes it into the narrowest limits, if it does not nullify it altogether.

On the roads operated by the Louisville & Nashville Railroad Company the maximum legal rates authorized by the charter vary from 7 to 10.2 cents per ton per mile. The average actual charge made is 2.172 cents. Why does not the company charge more, having an undoubted right to do so? Other causes than the mere will of the managers limit the charges. In one case it is competition, in another the freight is of such a character that it can not bear higher charges, or both of these causes are in operation at the same time.

I can assert from my personal experience that on 920 miles of railroads, stretching in all directions over a large territory of country, the managers have no more to do with the making of the tariffs than to study the conditions and limitations to which I have referred, and to conform to the same. The result is that the tariff charges on these roads are but from 20 to 30 per cent of the maximum authorized by law. I can also affirm that a similar state of affairs exists in regard to the large number of railroads with whose affairs I am acquainted.

If the mere will of the managers, unchecked by other considerations, had absolute control over railroad tariffs, would it be likely that so many roads in the United States would be in the hands of receivers; so many more unable to pay dividends to stockholders; so comparatively few paying the usual interest on the cost of construction; and so few paying a larger interest?

Any one who asserts that the railroads in this country as a whole are guilty of extortion only shows his own ignorance of the facts, easily accessible, and exhibited by the statistics in regard to the financial result of railroad operation in the United States. The truth is that the people of this country are furnished with transportation for less than its cost, at the expense of the owners of railroad property.

The general practice of citing one or two cases of unreasonable railroad charges, or a few cases where railroad companies pay dividends upon watered stock, and basing upon this the charge that all or the great majority of railroads in the country are doing this, is manifestly unjust. If the charge is made against the railroad system as a whole, it stands refuted by the general result of its operations as a whole.

That errors are committed by railroad managers in arranging their tariffs, especially in details, can not be denied (and this is equally true in other important human avocations), nor can it be wondered at, if we bear in mind the complications and difficulties of this work. But as the interests which are intended to be served necessarily suffer from these errors, it should be presumed that they are the result of ignorance rather than evil intent, and the only correction in this matter is better information, sounder judgment, and greater intelligence. If these requirements could be supplied by legislation, the end would be accomplished. Much might be done by instituting intelligent inquiry and investigation of the facts bearing upon the subject, and by disseminating the result among the people. In this direction legislative influence should first be exercised.

GOVERNMENTAL RAILROAD TARIFFS A FAILURE.

The foregoing consideration of the subject of legislative control of railroad property leads to the following conclusions.

First, that such control can not be exercised by general laws establishing fixed railroad tariffs without a violation of the rights of the parties owning the property.

Second, that it is impossible under such fixed railroad tariffs to fully develop the usefulness of railroads to their owners and the people.

The experience of the past regarding special railroad legislation confirms the correctness of these conclusions.

Mr. Charles F. Adams sums up the result of his thorough investigations of the subject of governmental interference with railroad tariffs in the report of the railroad commissioners to the legislature of the state of Massachusetts. Referring especially to Great Britain, he says, "Nowhere has the system of special legislation been more persistently followed, and nothing, it may be added, could have been more complete than its failure."

And again: "The result of thirty years of successive and wholly abortive efforts in this direction in England has been that Parliament has at last settled down in the conviction that the developments and necessities of trade in practice always have nullified, and inevitably must nullify, the special acts, no matter how carefully and skillfully they may be prepared."

PREVENTION OF EXTORTION AND UNJUST DISCRIMINATION.

It is only surprising that it should have required thirty years to establish a fact that must appear evident at once if we thoroughly analyze the nature of the object sought to be attained, and the instruments and means available for its attainment, and still more surprising when we consider that the object of all the efforts referred to could be simply reached by enforcing the *common law*, which *prohibits common carriers from making unreasonable charges* for transportation.

Let the parties guilty of a violation of this law alone be held responsible. This course has been deemed sufficient heretofore to prevent wrong-doing, and if followed and adhered to, should also be sufficient to prevent extortion on the part of railroad companies.

It has been urged against the efficiency of the law that the expense of litigation deters individuals from seeking redress. To remove this objection the state could provide an indictment against offending railroad companies, and throw the cost of litigation upon the commonwealth. It has also been urged that it is difficult, if not impossible, to make proof of the unreasonableness of railroad charges. Several plans have been proposed to remove this objection.

The House of Representatives of the United States proposed a law by which nine commissioners were to guess at the rates which should be considered reasonable. I say *guess*, because it would be entirely impossible for nine men to ascertain what are reasonable rates, upon correct principles, for all roads in the United States.

The legislatures of some states have adopted arbitrary tariffs, which are to be considered reasonable until proved otherwise. The object of these measures is simply to throw the burden of proof as to the reasonableness of transportation charges upon the railroad companies.

F

But in so doing it raises fictitious issues; it declares certain things reasonable which are not so, and makes an untruth the basis upon which a legal action is to be brought.

It is difficult to perceive why all this complicated machinery was invented to reach an object that can be simply reached by enacting a law which shall throw at once the burden of proof upon the railroad companies. Such a law would be perfectly just and proper. It is the business of the common carrier to know when he establishes a tariff that it is in accordance with the requirements of law; and having all the facts bearing upon the question in his possession, he should have no difficulty in making the proof.

A rigid and frequent application of the law as above suggested to railroad carriers would soon prove whether the many complaints made are based upon facts or upon fiction. The judicial investigation in a number of cases, aided by the testimony of experts in railroad management, would soon bring to light and establish the proper principle upon which questions as to extortionate rates and unjust discriminations should be decided; and it would not be long before people would learn to understand and look upon the subject in its proper light.

The present persecution of railroads, which in some parts of the country has become a mania, is not unlike the persecution of witchcraft in former years. It must cease as soon as intelligence has taken the place of ignorance. When this point has been reached many of the supposed difficulties of the railroad problem will be solved.

It has been with a view of contributing something toward this desirable end that I have discussed the subject in this report at so great length.

CONTENTS OF TABLES OF ANNUAL REPORT.

I propose now, after having referred to the subject of railroad transportation in general, to complete the report of the operations of the Louisville & Nashville Railroad during the past year. The contents of tables I to XXV, relating to the expenditures, were referred to on pages 8 to 17. I wish now to refer to the remaining tables, from XXVI to XLV, containing information in regard to the tonnage and number of passengers transported, and the revenue derived therefrom, and showing also the sources from which the business is derived, character of the freight, etc.

Table XXVI shows the number of tons and ton-miles of local and through freight transported ; the total revenue received from freight ; also the revenue and the operating expenses per ton-mile on each road.

Table XXVII shows the number of tons of freight transported to and from each station, and the number of tons carried one mile.

Table XXVIII shows the quantity and kind of freight forwarded from each station.'

Table XXIX shows the total quantity of each kind of freight forwarded from all stations of each road during the past and preceding years.

Table XXX shows the quantity and kind of freight received at each station.

Table XXXI shows the quantities and kind of freight received at Louisville from each station on the various roads.

Table XXXII shows the total quantity of each kind of freight received at Louisville during the past and preceding year.

Table XXXIII shows the quantity and kind of freight forwarded to each station of the road from Louisville.

Table XXXIV shows the quantity of each kind of freight forwarded from Louisville during the years 1872–3 and 1873–4.

Table XXXV shows the number of bales of cotton carried to and from Memphis, and from stations on Memphis & Ohio Railroad.

Table XXXVI shows the revenue from freight and passengers at each station of the road, and the tons of freight and number of passengers carried one mile from and to each station.

Table XXXVII shows the tonnage of and revenue from freight carried between Louisville and Nashville, coming from or destined to Louisville and all points North, or coming from or destined to Nashville and all points South.

Table XXXVIII shows the tonnage of and revenue from freight carried between Louisville, Memphis, and all junction points on the Memphis Line, arriving from and destined to Louisville, Memphis, and points beyond.

Table XXXIX shows the tonnage and revenue from freight coming from and going to points between Louisville and Montgomery and junction points.

Table XL shows the tonnage and revenue from freight between Nashville and Montgomery.

The preceding tables contain full information in regard to the competitive freight business, the sources from which derived, and its value to the company. The rates at which each separate class of business is carried and the net profits derived from each can be ascertained, and the question decided how profitable it is to the company or when it ceases to be so.

Table XLII shows the number of miles traveled by local and through passengers, and the average revenue per mile.

Table XLIII shows the number of local passengers on Main Stem and branches, and revenue derived from same on each road. This table shows the interchange of local passenger traffic between the various roads.

Table XLIV gives the same information in regard to both local and through passenger traffic.

Table XLV shows the proportion of revenue derived from freight business upon each road originating upon the other roads.

ESTIMATES OF THE VALUE OF BRANCH ROADS TO MAIN LINE.

From tables XLIV and XLV we are enabled to make estimates of the value of the branch roads and extensions of' the main line as feeders to it. One of the principal feeders is the Memphis Line. Its business passes over 118 miles of the Main Stem.

From Table XLIV it appears that the gross earnings of the Main Stem from passenger business coming from or going to the Memphis Line are $145,995.40. At 29.13 per cent the net earnings of the Main Stem—its total net earnings on account of this business—were.. 42,528 46

From Table XLV it appears that the gross freight earnings on the Main Stem derived from that line were $368,588.69, and net earnings, 39.20 per cent.............. 144,486 76

Total net earnings derived on Main Stem from business of the Memphis Line...................................... $187,015.12

The value of the Nashville & Decatur and South & North Alabama Railroads to the Main Stem as feeders may be estimated as follows:

Table XLIV shows the gross passenger earnings on the Main Stem derived from business on

Nashville & Decatur Railroad.. 19,537 36
South & North Alabama Railroad... 28,673 04

Total.. $48,210 40

As no extra trains are run on the Main Stem to accommodate this passenger' business, the whole of this may be considered as net earnings.

The gross earnings from freight business on the Main Stem

Coming from or going to the Nashville & Decatur Railroad are........... 52,763 73
From South and North Alabama Railroad..................................... 223,691 28

$276,455 01

And the net earnings from this business (39.20 per ct.), $108,370.36. The total net earnings of Main Stem increased by these two roads are $156,580.76.

The value of the Knoxville and Richmond Branches as feeders to the Main Stem may be estimated as follows:

Proportion of gross passenger earnings on Main Stem from business coming from or going to these two branches (Table XLIV) on $36,937.42 at 29.13 per cent net profit is..... .... 10,759 87
Proportion of gross freight earnings (Table XLV), $102,279.47, at 39.20 per cent....................... .... 40,093 55

Total net earnings on Main Stem derived from business of these two branch roads........................,......................... 50,853 42
Add this to the net earnings of these two branches........................... 86,563 14

The total net earnings of these two branches............... .... $137,416 56

The value of the Bardstown Branch as a feeder to the Main Stem is as follows:

Main Stem proportion of passenger earnings (Table XLIV), $10,775.53, at 29.13 per cent.. 3,138 91
Freight earnings (Table XLV), $16,915.65, at 39.20 per cent.............. 6,630 93

9,776 84
Add to this the net earnings of the Bardstown Branch itself................ 5,338 06

Total net earnings... $15,107 90

The value of the Glasgow Branch as a feeder to the Main Stem is as follows:

Proportion of passenger earnings on the Main Stem from business from the Glasgow Branch (Table XLIV)................................... 12,181 08
No additional trains are run to accommodate this business, and the whole amount may be considered as net earnings.
Proportion of freight earnings, as per Table XLV, $28,843.68; net profit 39.20 per cent... 11,306 72

Total.. $23,487 80

Recapitulating the results of the above estimates, we have the proportion of the net earnings which the Main Stem has derived from the business of the extension and branches as follows:

From Memphis Line	187,015 22
From Nashville & Decatur and South & North Alabama Railroads	156,580 76
From Knoxville and Richmond branches	50,853 42
From Bardstown Branch	9,769 84
From Glasgow Branch	11,306 72
Total	415,525 96
The total net earnings of the Main Stem were	896,244 64

Showing that without the branch roads and extensions the net revenue of the Main Stem would have been only $480,718 68

But we must consider that in the above estimate of the net earnings we have only taken the average net earnings. The large amount of business thrown on the Main Stem by these feeders has greatly reduced the operating expenses. The reduction so made may be estimated as follows:

The operating expenses on the Main Stem were 63.8 per cent of the gross earnings. The operating expenses on account of the $415,525.96 net earnings derived on the Main Stem from the business of the branch roads can therefore be estimated at $\frac{63.8}{36.2} \times$ $415,525.96 = $732,335.81$.

Twenty per cent of these expenses belong to that class which are fixed and independent of the amount of business (see Table A, p. 20, interest excluded), so that without the business that was brought to the Main Stem by its feeders the expenses of transacting the other business would have been increased by $732,335.81 \times \frac{20}{100}$ 146,467 16

Add to this the net earnings as above estimated 415,525 96

We have the total net earnings of the Main Stem on account of the branch roads and extension $561,993 12

This estimate shows that branch roads and extensions, although they may not be profitable in themselves, may become so by the influence they exercise upon the net revenue of the main line. It may occur even that a whole system of roads—main line and branches—is not remunerative, yet the final financial result that must be considered the test of the judiciousness of the investment in branch roads—*the proportion of the net revenue to the capital invested*—may be greater with than without the branches. It is therefore not possible to judge correctly of the judiciousness of such investments unless correct estimates can be made showing the net earnings directly and indirectly obtained on account of branch roads and extensions.

HEADING OF ACCOUNTS.

FROM TABLES II AND III.

— — —

. — — —

MAINTENANCE OF ROADWAY AND
GENERAL SUPERINTENDENCE.

Road Repairs per Mile of Road—
1 Adjustment of track.
2 Ballast.
3 Ditching.
4 Culverts and cattle-guards.
5 Extraordinary repairs—slides, etc.
6 Repairs of hand and dump-cars.
7 Repairs of road tools.
8 Road watchmen.
9 General expense of road department.
10 Total.
11 Cross-ties replaced—value.
12 Cross-ties, labor replacing.
13 Cross-ties, train expenses hauling.
14 Total cost of cross-ties per mile of road.
15 Bridge superstructure repairs.
16 Bridge watchmen.
17 Shop-building repairs.
18 Water-station repairs.
19 Section-house repairs.
20 Total cost of bridge and building repairs per mile of road.
21 General superintendence and general expense of operating department.
22 Advertising and soliciting passengers and freight.
23 Insurance and taxes.
24 Rent account.
25 Total per mile of road.
26 Salaries of general officers.
27 Insurance and taxes and general expense.
28 Total per mile of road.
29 *Total cost per mile of road for maintenance of roadway and buildings.*
29½ Total cost per train mile for maintenance of roadway and buildings.

STATION EXPENSES PER TRAIN MILE.

30 Labor loading and unloading freight.
31 Agents and clerks.
32 Gen'l expense of stations—lights, fuel, etc.
33 Watchmen and switchmen.
34 { *Expense of Switching*—Engine repairs.
   Engineers and firemen's wages.
   Expense in engine-house.
   Supervision and general expense.
   Oil and waste.
   Water supply.
   Fuel.

35 Total per train mile.
36 Stationery and printing.
37 Telegraph expenses.
38 Depot repairs.
39 Total per train mile.
40 *Total station expenses per train mile.*

MOVEMENT EXPENSES PER TRAIN
MILE.

41 Adjustment of track.
42 Cost of renewal of rails—value.
43 Labor replacing rails.
44 Train expenses hauling rails.
45 Joint Fastenings.
46 Switches.
47 Total cost of adjustment of track and replacing rails per train mile.
48 Locomotive repairs.
49 Oil and waste used on locomotives.
50 Watching and cleaning.
51 Fuel used in engine-house.
52 Supervision and general expense in engine-house.
53 Engineers and firemen's wages.
54 Total engine expenses per train mile.
55 Conductors and brakemen.
56 Passenger-car repairs.
57 Sleeping-car repairs.
58 Freight-car repairs.
59 Oil and waste used by cars.
60 Labor oiling and inspecting cars.
61 Train expenses.
62 Total car expenses per train mile.
63 Fuel used by locomotives.
64 Water supply.
65 Total fuel and water expense per train mile.
66 Damage to freight, and lost baggage.
67 Damage to stock.
68 Wrecking account.
69 Damage to persons.
70 Gratuity to employees.
71 Fencing burned.
72 Law expenses.
73 Total per train mile.
74 *Total movement expenses per train mile.*
75 GRAND TOTAL for maintenance and movement per train mile.

FORMULA FOR ASCERTAINING THE COST OF RAILROAD TRANSPORTATION PER TON-MILE;

SHOWING ALSO, WITH REFERENCE TO THE ITEMS OF EXPENDITURES ON PAGE 47, THE VARIOUS ELEMENTS ENTERING INTO THE CALCULATION OF COST.

Movement expenses per ton-mile $= \dfrac{\text{Movement expenses per train mile (items 41 to 74)}}{\text{average number of tons of freight in each train}} = a.$

Station expenses per ton-mile . $= \dfrac{\text{Cost of handling freight (items 30 to 40) at forwarding station} + \text{at delivery station}}{\text{length of haul}} = b.$

Maintenance of road per ton-mile $= \dfrac{\text{Cost of maintenance of road per mile per year (items 1 to 29)} \times \frac{\text{total miles run by freight-trains per year}}{\text{total revenue trains, pass. and fr't, pr. yr.}}}{\text{average number of tons of freight transported over one mile of road per year}} = c.$

Interest per ton-mile . . . . $= \dfrac{\text{Cost of road per mile} \times \frac{\text{rate of interest per annum}}{100} \times \frac{\text{number of freight-train miles per year}}{\text{number of revenue-train miles, fr't and pass, per year}}}{\text{average number of tons of freight transported over one mile of road per year}} = d.$

Total cost per ton-mile $= a + b + c + d.$

In order to make use of this formula it is necessary to know the fifty-eight items of expense enumerated on page 47, all of which vary on different roads, and enter into different combinations with each other. Some of the items of movement expenses (41 to 74) change with the weight of trains, and have to be ascertained in each individual case. The average cost for the year can be made the basis of the estimate. Besides the items shown on page 47, the following other items enter into the calculation : the average number of tons of freight in train per mile of the round trip of the train, the average length of haul, the number of miles run over the road with freight and passenger-trains per annum, the cost of the road, the rate of interest, and the total number of tons of freight carried during a year over one mile of road. Without these data it is impossible to make a correct estimate of the cost of transportation on railroads.